AF580954

KINGFISHER
LONDON & NEW YORK

First published in 2026 in the United States by Kingfisher
120 Broadway, New York, NY 10271
Kingfisher is an imprint of
Macmillan Children's Books, London

Distributed in the U.S. and Canada by Macmillan,
120 Broadway, New York, NY 10271

Library of Congress Cataloging-in-Publication Data has been applied for

ISBN 978-0-7534-8184-4

Printed in China
10 9 8 7 6 5 4 3 2 1

EU representative: Macmillan Publishers Ireland Ltd, 1st Floor,
The Liffey Trust Centre, 117-126 Sheriff Street Upper, Dublin 1 D01 YC43

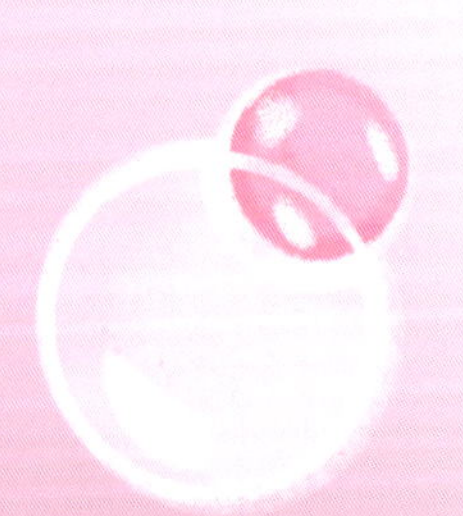

Let's Meet
ARIANA

ILLUSTRATED BY MARIANA AVILA LAGUNES
WRITTEN BY CLAIRE BAKER

On a sunny Florida day in June 1993, Joan Grande and Ed Butera celebrated the arrival of their baby girl, Ariana.

Big brother Frankie was delighted! So was Marjorie, Ariana's Italian grandmother, or nonna.

The whole family loved music. They enjoyed singing karaoke at home . . .

. . . and watching musicals.
Ariana's favorite was *The Wizard of Oz.*

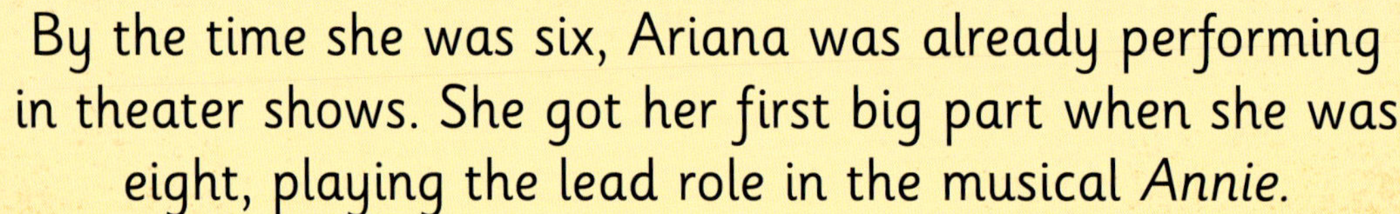

By the time she was six, Ariana was already performing in theater shows. She got her first big part when she was eight, playing the lead role in the musical *Annie.*

Ariana's mom wanted to keep an eye on her at the theater, so she got a part too, as an apple seller.

Ariana enjoyed acting, but she loved singing the most. She was still only eight when she sang the national anthem at a Florida Panthers hockey game.

By the time she was twelve, Ariana had written her first song, "Let It Rain," even though she didn't have a recording deal yet.

She also helped create a group of young singers that raised over half a million dollars to help children in need.

At fifteen, Ariana won a role in a musical at a theater on Broadway. Now it was time to leave Florida and live in New York for a few months.

At sixteen, Ariana was on the move again, this time to Los Angeles. There she starred in a television show called "Victorious," which was filmed in Hollywood.

The show was set in a performing arts school, so Ariana got plenty of chances to sing.

Her character, Cat, had bright red hair—but Ariana didn't! She had to dye it every two weeks instead.

Ariana enjoyed singing on the soundtrack albums for "Victorious" with the other young actors from the show. But she still dreamed of singing her own favorite type of music too.

When she wasn't at the television studio, Ariana recorded herself singing songs by famous female singers. Then she posted the videos online.

Luckily a record company executive saw them, and at last Ariana's dream came true—she signed a recording contract!

Ariana was eighteen when she released her first single, "Put Your Hearts Up." She let her fans vote on which cover design she should pick for it.

Now she was ready to record her first solo album.

When the show “Victorious” came to an end, Ariana’s character appeared in a spin-off series. Now she wore wigs instead of dyeing her hair all the time.

When that show ended, Ariana acted in other television and theater shows. She also started singing the kind of music she loved the most.

It had taken nearly three years to record, but at last Ariana's first album was ready for release. It was called *Yours Truly*, and it shot straight to number one.

Ariana sang songs from the album on her first mini tour, performing in U.S. cities.

The following year, the president of the United States invited Ariana to sing at the White House. She participated in a concert to celebrate female musicians.

Later that year, Ariana released her second album—and now it was time for her to go on her first big world tour!

The tour began in the U.S. in February 2015 and ended in Brazil eight months later.

Ariana had sung and danced her way around the world, performing at 81 concerts in 20 different countries.

Now Ariana was a real star, with devoted fans who called themselves Arianators. She kept herself busy . . .

. . . recording more songs and touring . . .

. . . hosting a popular American TV show . . .

. . . singing at a huge festival in California . . .

. . . and winning lots of awards.

By the time she was 28 years old, Ariana had released six hit albums and sold millions of records all around the world.

She sometimes sang duets with other famous singers too.

But it wasn't all music! Ariana also launched some fragrances and then a makeup brand too.

With so much to do, Ariana knows it's important to slow down sometimes.

Reading her favorite books helps. . .

So does taking time to meditate.

She likes to write in her journal too.

Ariana also enjoys hearing from her fans and spending time with her family.

Her parents and big brother Frankie always support her when they can.

It's not just people that Ariana cares about. She's also adopted quite a few rescue dogs of all shapes and sizes.

Sometimes she even brings the smaller ones with her when she's working!

Ariana doesn't just write songs—she also wrote, directed, and starred in a short film. Her own dad even played her father.

To win her dream part in the movie *Wicked*, Ariana took extra acting and singing lessons.

It paid off, and Ariana got a starring role as Glinda, the good witch, who is also a character in her favorite musical, *The Wizard of Oz.*

Ariana loves singing and acting, but she also stands up for what she believes in and speaks out when she thinks something isn't right.

She supports good causes too, like sending presents to children who are spending Christmas in the hospital.

Most of all, Ariana lives by the rules her mom taught her when she was young: be kind, work hard, and only worry about the things that really matter.

That's what's made her such a superstar with millions of fans all around the world!